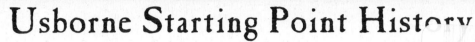

What were castles for?

Phil Roxbee Cox

Illustrated by Sue Stitt & Annabel Spenceley

Designed by Diane Thistlethwaite & Vicki Groombridge

Series editor: Jane Chisholm

History consultant: Dr. Anne Millard

Cover illustration: Gerald Wood

CONTENTS

Usborne Quicklinks

For links to websites where you can find out lots more
about castles and castle life, go to the Usborne Quicklinks website at
www.usborne.com/quicklinks and type in the keywords **starting castles**.
Please follow the internet safety guidelines displayed at the Usborne Quicklinks website.

What were castles for?

Castles were places for lords and their families to live in. They were built to keep out enemies and to keep people, horses and treasures safe.

Castles were also important as bases where lords could keep knights and horses to ride out and fight off enemy attacks.

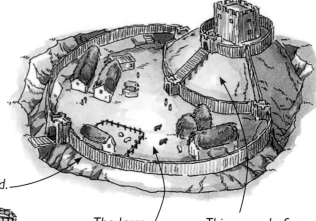

This is what some of the very early castles looked like. This type of castle is called a motte and bailey.

All the fences and walls are built of wood.

The large courtyard is called the bailey.

This mound of earth was called the motte.

This huge castle was built in the Middle East in the 13th century.

Thick stone walls

Battlements

This fortress was built on Egypt's southern border around 4,000 years ago.

What did castles look like?

Very different from each other. Early stone castles had just one square tower in the middle, called a keep. Later castles were made up of many buildings.

Castles have been around for a very long time, but the great age of castle-building was in the Middle Ages. Most of the castles in this book come from then.

What and when were the Middle Ages?

The name later given to a period of European history. Things that happened in, or come from, the Middle Ages are called "medieval".

The Middle Ages started around the year 900 (the 10th century) and ended around 1500 (the 16th century). A century is a hundred years. The 10th century lasted from 901 to 1000, and so on. So medieval castles developed and changed over a period of about 600 years.

This Japanese fortress was built in the 17th century.

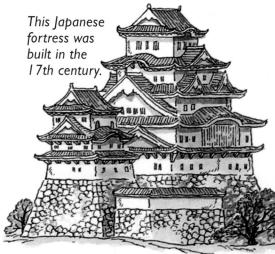

2

Who built them?

Kings, princes, lords and landowners had castles built. Skilled and unskilled workers actually built them. Skilled workers included stone carvers, called stone masons. Unskilled workers did all the pulling, pushing and lifting.

Where were castles built?

In areas where land needed to be protected from enemies. Once it had been decided to build a castle, the best site was chosen. Castles needed a supply of water, a good view of surrounding land and as much natural protection as possible. Castles were often built on hills for defence. Some castles added a moat.

What was a moat?

A wide, deep ditch full of water running all the way around a castle. A moat was dug to keep out unwanted visitors. People were only let in across a well-guarded bridge.

A moat made it very difficult for an attacking army to tunnel under the castle's walls. The tunnel would fill with water.

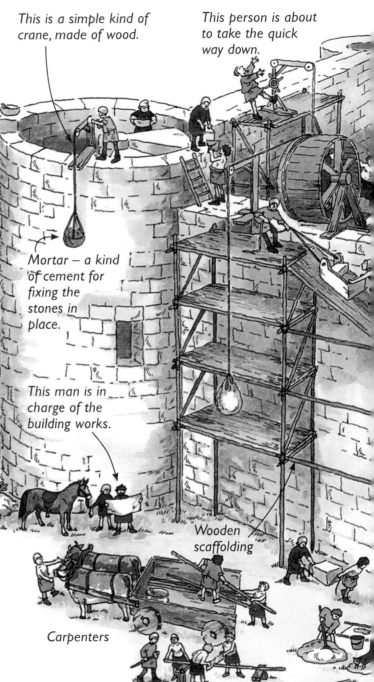

This scene shows men building a castle in Europe in the Middle Ages.

This is a simple kind of crane, made of wood.

This person is about to take the quick way down.

Mortar – a kind of cement for fixing the stones in place.

This man is in charge of the building works.

Stones arriving from the quarry

A worried worker

This man is learning to be a mason.

A wobbly wheel

Wooden scaffolding

Carpenters

What did they keep in a keep?

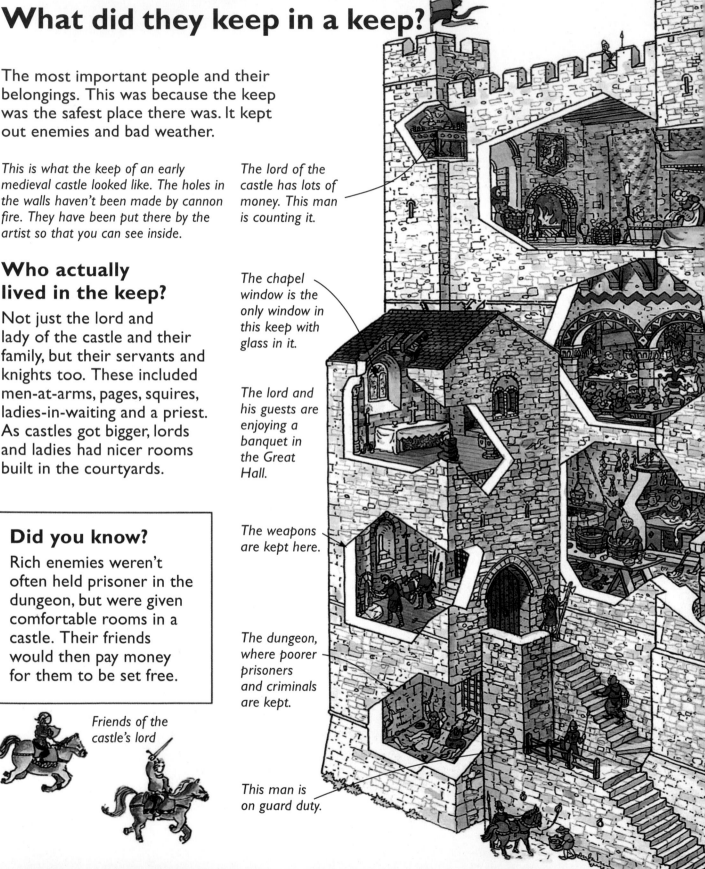

The most important people and their belongings. This was because the keep was the safest place there was. It kept out enemies and bad weather.

This is what the keep of an early medieval castle looked like. The holes in the walls haven't been made by cannon fire. They have been put there by the artist so that you can see inside.

Who actually lived in the keep?

Not just the lord and lady of the castle and their family, but their servants and knights too. These included men-at-arms, pages, squires, ladies-in-waiting and a priest. As castles got bigger, lords and ladies had nicer rooms built in the courtyards.

Did you know?

Rich enemies weren't often held prisoner in the dungeon, but were given comfortable rooms in a castle. Their friends would then pay money for them to be set free.

The lord of the castle has lots of money. This man is counting it.

The chapel window is the only window in this keep with glass in it.

The lord and his guests are enjoying a banquet in the Great Hall.

The weapons are kept here.

The dungeon, where poorer prisoners and criminals are kept.

This man is on guard duty.

Friends of the castle's lord

This is a garderobe, a medieval castle toilet.

The kitchens are full of servants sweating away to prepare the food.

There weren't any fridges or freezers, so food that needed to be kept cold was kept in the coldest room down here.

Casks of wine

Did they have toilets?

Sort of. There were pots in the lord and lady's bed chamber, which is how they came to be called chamber pots. Servants had to empty them.

There were also things called garderobes. These were seats above chutes set in the outer walls of the keep.

Where do you think . . . ?

Where do you think that the waste from the garderobe went? What problems might this have caused?

Where did they sleep?

The rich had cosy beds with curtains around them. The servants were not so lucky. They had to bring out their thin straw mattresses and sleep wherever they could. This was often in the Great Hall.

Did they have baths?

Yes, baths were tubs like barrels. Some of these were so big that people needed steps to climb into them.

Even the noblest of nobles didn't have baths very often. The tubs were carried into the bedroom when they were wanted.

A servant carries buckets of hot water from the kitchen to the lord's bedchamber.

What went on inside the castle walls?

It depends. A castle was its lord's home. It was a place to collect the rents, taxes and food he gathered from his lands. But, in times of trouble, it was also where his people would go for protection.

After a time, people stopped building keeps. Rooms were built into castle walls.

Who could live inside the walls?

As well as the nobles and servants, there were armourers, smiths, fletchers, ostlers, falconers and dog handlers. Armourers made armour and weapons. Smiths made horseshoes, nails and other things. Fletchers made arrows. Ostlers looked after the horses. Falconers trained birds called falcons.

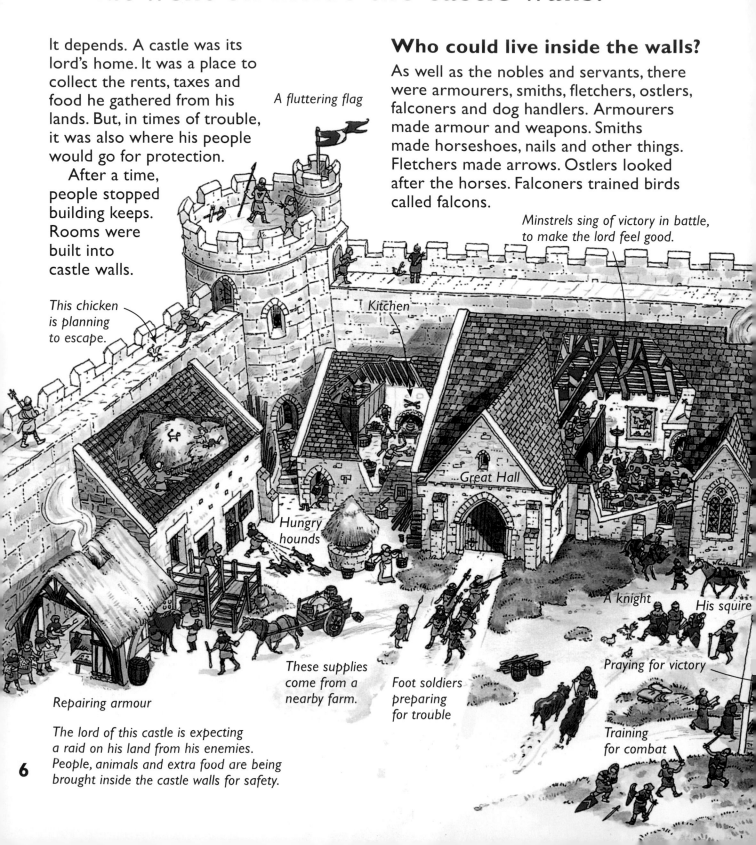

A fluttering flag

Minstrels sing of victory in battle, to make the lord feel good.

This chicken is planning to escape.

Kitchen

Great Hall

Hungry hounds

A knight

His squire

Praying for victory

These supplies come from a nearby farm.

Foot soldiers preparing for trouble

Repairing armour

Training for combat

The lord of this castle is expecting a raid on his land from his enemies. People, animals and extra food are being brought inside the castle walls for safety.

6

What farm animals did they keep?

Very few. Most farm animals were kept on farms. But they might keep chickens, geese and ducks inside the walls.

Some castles had lofts full of pigeons too. If a castle was under siege, larger animals would be brought inside for protection.

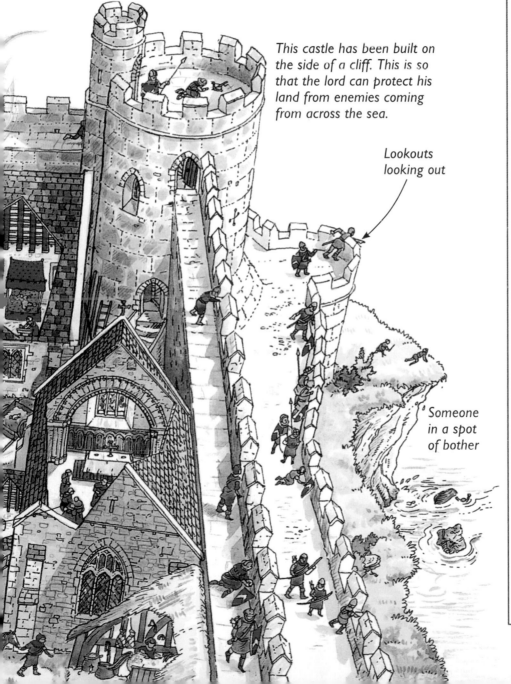

This castle has been built on the side of a cliff. This is so that the lord can protect his land from enemies coming from across the sea.

Lookouts looking out

Someone in a spot of bother

What is a drawbridge?

The answer is best explained with pictures.

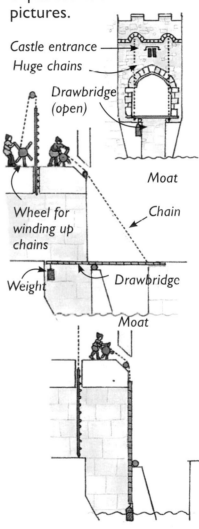

Castle entrance

Huge chains

Drawbridge (open)

Moat

Wheel for winding up chains

Chain

Weight

Drawbridge

Moat

This last picture shows the chains wound right up so that the drawbridge is now closed. The bridge has now become a huge closed door. This leaves no easy way to cross the moat, which helps to keep the enemy out.

What did nobles do for fun?

Noblemen and noblewomen enjoyed eating big meals, listening to stories and songs, watching jousts (see pages 24-25) and hunting. Later, dancing became popular too.

How did nobles hunt?

They would always be on horseback. Servants known as huntsmen ran alongside them to help manage the animals. Sometimes nobles hunted with a pack of hounds, and sometimes they enjoyed a different kind of hunting called falconry.

This scene shows a medieval deer hunt. You may be pleased to know that, this time, only one will get caught. The hunt is taking place in the land belonging to the lord of the castle.

There is someone up this tree. He is hiding, which is why you can't see him.

Traps for catching rabbits

A noble. That is why he is on a horse.

What did they hunt?

Stags, bears, wolves, wild boar, deer, rabbits and birds were all popular victims.

Poor people often hunted on their lord's land too, usually for something to eat. This wasn't allowed and was called poaching. If they were caught, they were given horrible punishments.

This stag is about to make a clean getaway.

What is falconry?

Using specially trained birds, called falcons, to catch and bring back small animals.

Falconry was very popular with both lords and ladies.

This horse is stopping for a quick bite to eat.

Wild boar hiding from the hunters

These ladies are enjoying themselves with their falcons.

A trained falcon

Tapestry of a hunting scene

What else did women do for fun?

Embroidery was very popular, but shouldn't be muddled with tapestry. A noblewoman would embroider small items such as cushion covers. Tapestries were much bigger and usually made by weavers.

This noble lady is embroidering a cushion cover. It's rather good.

How was a falcon trained?

With a lot of hard work, care and patience.

Falconer

Falcon

Thick glove

The bird learns that its food comes from its master.

The bird learns to wear a hood, covering its eyes.

Leather rein

With the hood off, but on a rein, the falcon flies after scraps of food thrown in the air.

Bird killed by falcon

Finally, the falcon flies free, attacking small birds, then returning to the falconer. Now it is ready for a nobleman or woman to take out hunting.

Who or what were knights?

All knights were men, but very few men were knights. You had to be "of noble birth" and train as a page and a squire first. (See over the page.)

A knight swore to be faithful to his king and to serve God. He was also supposed to protect the weak.

A knight was addressed with "Sir" in front of his name. To be recognized easily, he had a coat of arms on his shield.

What did knights wear?

In battle and tournaments, knights wore armour. The first armour was made of thick leather, and links of metal called chainmail.

Later, it was made up of very tough pieces of metal fixed together with joints.

This is called a morning star. It's about to make a dent in the other man's head, as well as his helmet.

Every knight had his own unique coat of arms. You can find out more about these below.

Knights' horses were big and chunky like these two. They had to be, to carry the weight of a knight in full armour.

What is a coat of arms?

A design made up of special pictures and symbols.

Every rich family had one. They wore it on their clothes, armour and shields so that people could recognize them in battle. When people had their helmets on, it was difficult to tell who was who.

Some simple coats of arms

Did armour rust in the wet?

Yes, if it wasn't looked after properly. It was the job of a knight's squire and pages to make sure it didn't rust. Everything had to be oiled and polished.

By rolling the barrel, this page is making the sand brush against his master's chainmail. This should rub off any rust.

A sweaty page

Chainmail

Sand

Barrel

Who were the Knights of the Round Table?

Old British legends tell of a great king named Arthur. He lived in a castle called Camelot. There, he and his knights would sit and make plans at a huge round table. Because of this, King Arthur's knights were known as the Knights of the Round Table.

Did they really exist?

Arthur probably did, and he would have had men fighting for him. They would not have dressed like the knights in this book, though. They came from the much earlier time of around 500.

Pictures of King Arthur, like this one, often show him in a kind of armour the real king would never have seen.

More coats of arms

Can I design my own coat of arms?

Good idea. You could make up a pretend one using some of the designs on these pages.

In some countries, there are still strict rules about what you can and cannot put on your coat of arms.

11

Who could be a knight?

Men who came from "good" (rich) families, and who had gone through the hard training of being first a page, then a squire. Women couldn't become knights. Neither could men from ordinary families.

This boy is going off to his uncle's castle to be a page.

Jealous sister

Sad but proud parents

These pages are listening to stories of battles lost and won.

Abacus

This page is trying to do simple sums, using something called an abacus.

Lord   Lady

Part of a page's job is to serve his lord and lady's meals at table.

Meal

A tablecloth in need of a good wash

What was a page?

The first stage of getting to be a knight. Boys were usually sent away from home to become pages. They learned good manners, trained with weapons and were given a basic education.

Did pages learn to read and write?

In the early days, no one bothered. All knights wanted to do was to beat each other in battle. There seemed no point in being able to read or write. Later, this changed and pages were taught both.

This is the best shot so far.

This page had better move out of the way.

This boy is learning to shoot with a crossbow. He hasn't managed to hit the target yet.

Squires

This squire is an excellent horseman. He has to be strong to carry the weight of the armour he will wear.

Young squires helping a knight put on his armour.

What did squires have to do?

Look after their knights, from helping them get dressed to caring for their weapons and horses. They also learned to fight on horseback. This was the next stage after being a successful page.

How were squires knighted?

By the lord or king. He rested a sword on the squire's shoulders and declared him to be a knight. This was called "dubbing".

Coat of arms

The man in the armour is a squire who is going to be made a knight.

Now that this squire has become a knight, he is given a pair of spurs in another ceremony.

The lord knights the squire with a ceremonial sword.

This person is going to be knighted next.

Spurs

13

What weapons did people use?

It changed over time, but everything from rocks to bows and arrows, spear-like weapons and, later, guns and cannons. A rock could be very effective when dropped on someone's head. Proper cannons were not common until the 15th century.

Did they have guns?

Not really. There were a few very simple types of guns tried out as early as the 1320s, but they were pretty useless. They could not be fired accurately, and they could easily hurt the person firing them. So they didn't really become popular until much later.

Arrows fired from bows were much better at hitting their targets over long distances. So they were much more common.

Who used bows and arrows?

Ordinary soldiers, not knights. The most popular bows were held upright, and used to fire long, thin arrows. Crossbows fired shorter, heavier arrows or bolts.

Knights' most important weapons

were swords, lances and morning stars.

This army of soldiers is firing at their enemy across the valley. Only the man on the horse is a knight.

Longbows originally came from Wales. They soon became popular with English archers, too.

Pike staffs

A bang

Crossbow

A cross bowman

This boy is not a page – he is helping ordinary troops on the battlefield.

Loading a crossbow

This is an early type of cannon called a bombard.

This will be fired from the bombard.

Why did they use different bows?

Good question. Why do you think some soldiers used upright bows and some used crossbows? Have a think about what the reasons might be. (The answer is on page 32.)

A medieval picture of someone using a bow.

Bow

Did they have tanks?

Although the answer is 'no', this question isn't as silly as it sounds. Medieval soldiers did use something called a siege tower. This was a huge wooden structure, full of armed soldiers, which could be wheeled right up to the side of a castle wall.

What is a morning star?

Imagine a baton with a short chain at the top attached to a metal ball covered in spikes. The idea was for a knight to grip the baton and swing the chain around, so that the ball hit his enemy.

A morning star

A lance

This man is a sergeant at arms. He is telling the knight what has been happening.

Did you know?

We can tell what weapons and armour some noble knights used by studying their gravestones.

Some knights had pictures of themselves cut into brass and screwed onto their gravestones (which lay flat on the ground, not upright).

These pictures are called brasses.

A brass

Armour

Sword

Dagger

Shield

What was a castle feast like?

In good times, very filling and very noisy. What people ate depended on the period in history, the time of year and which country they were in. But wherever the feast was, whenever it was, you can be sure that there was plenty of drinking, laughing and shouting.

Where did they eat?

In the Great Hall. The most important guests and nobles sat at the "high table" with the lord and lady. Less important people sat on lower tables in front of them. Servants and peasants weren't usually invited to castle feasts.

A page serving

This swan has been plucked, cooked and then had all its feathers stuck back on.

This guest is unwell. Perhaps the stew didn't agree with him.

High table

A horn full of wine

People eat with their fingers and knives, but not forks.

A minstrel playing a lute

Most people are using slices of stale bread as plates. These will be given out to the poor later.

Scraps weren't supposed to be thrown on the floor, but they sometimes fell there anyway. That is why this dog looks happy.

This lower table isn't really a table, but planks resting on supports.

This boy is a young squire, training to be a knight. One of his tasks is to wait at the high table.

Bread ovens

Meat roasting on a spit

Servant roasting by the spit

Feeding the fire

An accident about to happen

As well as cutting apples for a pie, this boy has also cut his finger.

Boar's head (wild pig) — a popular dish

Ducks' eggs

A hungry rat

This picture shows part of a castle kitchen. Servants are hard at work preparing for a feast.

This cat is supposed to be catching rats.

What did nobles eat?

Usually meat, with fish on Fridays and salted meat in winter. The meat was stored in salt in autumn so that it would last. They didn't have fridges or freezers to keep food fresh. They also ate bread, eggs, cheese, vegetables and fruit.

Where was it cooked?

In the kitchens, of course. In some castles, like the one on page 5, the kitchens were in the keep. In other castles, the kitchens were in buildings in the courtyard.

How was it cooked?

Vegetables were boiled and meat was usually roasted on a huge spit in front of an open fire. The fat dripping from the meat was collected and spread on pieces of bread.

What is a famine?

When there isn't enough food to eat. This happened when crops didn't grow because of bad weather. Famine could also be caused by people's enemies destroying their food supply.

Where did people who didn't live in castles live?

In the countryside around the castle, or in villages. Most people were peasant farmers. Only a few owned the land they farmed. The rest rented land from the lord of the local castle. Not many lived in towns.

What were peasants' homes like?

Small and basic. Often cottages had only one room. The roofs were thatched, the floors were just earth, and there was no glass in the windows. The walls were often made of wattle-and-daub.

This village has been built near a river so that people can get their water from it.

Fed-up fisherman

Watermill

Church

A puddle

Pilgrims

Local fair

Vegetable garden

What is "wattle-and-daub"?

Wattle is a frame of wooden stakes with long twigs woven between them. Daub is mixture of clay, straw and dung that was smeared on top, to make a smooth, thick wall.

Wooden stakes

Woven twigs

Daub

18

A village wouldn't have both a windmill and a watermill. The artist has drawn both so that you can see what they look like.

The mill belonged to the lord. Peasants had to pay to use it.

A hungry wolf about to eat a thief about to attack a man on a horse

Windy washing

Inn

Stable

What did they do for a living?

Most people worked on the land. They grew crops and raised animals. In good times, they usually had just enough to live off. Most of what they produced was paid in taxes to the lord in his castle, and to the church.

What went on in a village?

People came in from the countryside to meet, find things they needed and go to church. Craftsmen such as carpenters, blacksmiths and potters lived there. Some villages also had a market where goods could be exchanged, and an inn where travellers could sleep.

Was it safe living in the country?

Not very. Hungry wolves in winter, and thieves on the road made the country quite a dangerous place. Villages didn't have the protection of high walls or guards.

19

There's more on the next page.

People who didn't live in the countryside, or in castles, lived in towns. Towns often grew up around castles. Over the centuries, many of these castles have fallen into ruin or gone completely, but the towns are still there.

Who lived in towns?

Mostly craftspeople, traders, merchants. and their families. People working in the same trade often lived in the same street. Craftspeople often set up societies called guilds.

Those who did't have craft skills had to settle for unpleasant jobs such as rat catching or collecting dung.

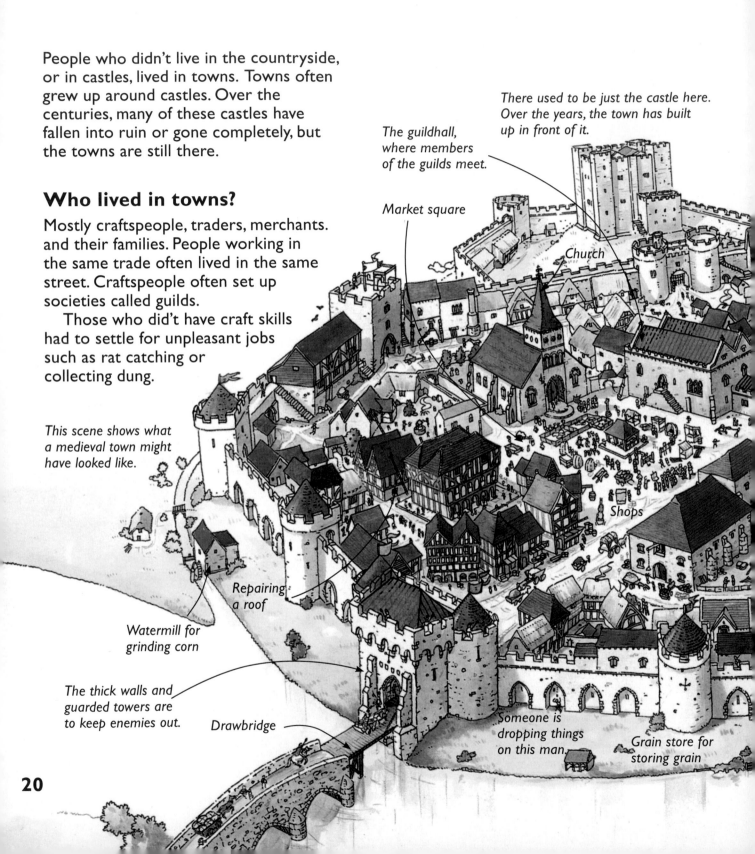

There used to be just the castle here. Over the years, the town has built up in front of it.

The guildhall, where members of the guilds meet.

Market square

Church

This scene shows what a medieval town might have looked like.

Shops

Repairing a roof

Watermill for grinding corn

The thick walls and guarded towers are to keep enemies out.

Drawbridge

Someone is dropping things on this man.

Grain store for storing grain

There's a monastery just over the hill. Find out more about monasteries on the next page.

Did they keep animals?

Not farm animals. They did keep horses, dogs and cats. Fleas, lice, mice and rats were also a common sight... not that people wanted them around! Some dogs probably caused trouble too.

Thatched roofs caught fire easily.

Above this gateway is a grand room which is used for meetings.

Hardly any houses have gardens. Most people buy vegetables at the market, or grow them beyond the town walls.

Were towns smelly?

Indeed they were. People didn't have washing machines, bathrooms or toilets. They slopped their waste into the street.

The houses in this part of town have tiled roofs, not thatched ones. This means that the richer people live here.

This wagon is full of things to sell at market, but it's hard to tell what.

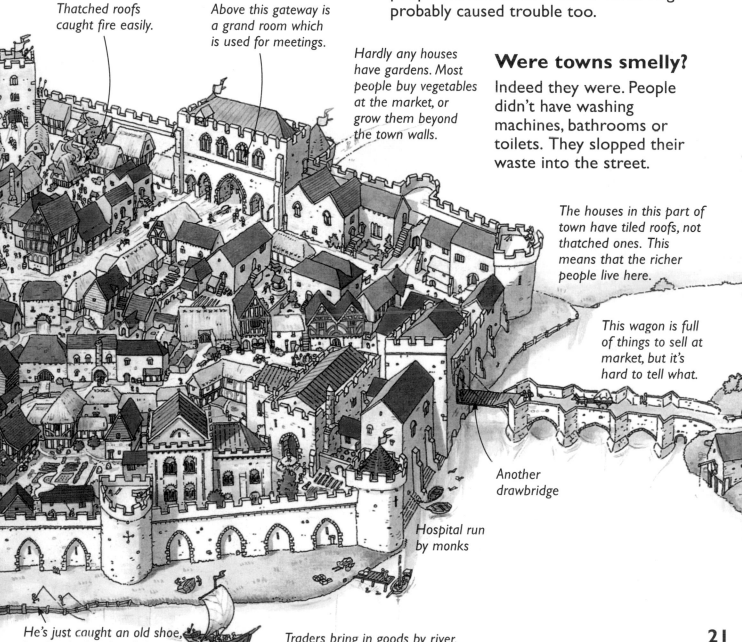

Another drawbridge

Hospital run by monks

He's just caught an old shoe, but he thinks it's a fish.

Traders bring in goods by river.

What was a monastery?

A building full of monks. These were men who had chosen to serve God in a special way. A nunnery was like a monastery, except that it was for women called nuns.

Monks and nuns made special promises called vows. They vowed not to own any property, not to marry and to obey the people in charge.

Who was in charge?

The Abbot or Prior or, in a nunnery, the Abbess or Prioress. Monasteries and nunneries followed strict rules, telling them how to live and when to pray. These were first made by a Christian saint called Benedict.

This picture is of a monastery. Some walls have been left out so that you can look inside.

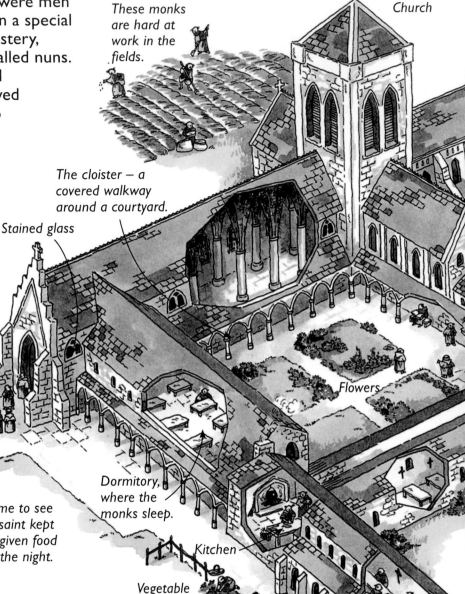

These monks are hard at work in the fields.

Church

The cloister – a covered walkway around a courtyard.

Stained glass

Flowers

People have come to see the bones of a saint kept here. They are given food and shelter for the night.

Dormitory, where the monks sleep.

Kitchen

Vegetable garden

How could you get to be a monk?

You had to be an unmarried man and a Christian. You started off as a novice. This meant that you had to follow the rules and learn the ways of the monastery.

Only then could you take your vows and become a true monk. Some people found this too hard. Others went on to spend their whole lives serving God.

What exactly did monks do?

Apart from worshipping privately and
together, they often nursed the sick,
taught, gave food and money to the poor
and tried to help people. Monks also
grew food, made beer, and kept bees.
It was a hard-working but peaceful life.

This picture from a 15th century manuscript
shows a woman writing a manuscript.

Monks on the move

Guesthouse

Abbot's house

The Abbot

Visitors

The chapter house,
where monks meet.

Did you know?

In the Middle Ages, very few people
could actually read or write. All early
Bibles and prayer books, as well as most
written records of events, were made
by monks or nuns. These were usually
beautifully decorated documents, written
with a pen called a quill. They are called
illuminated manuscripts.

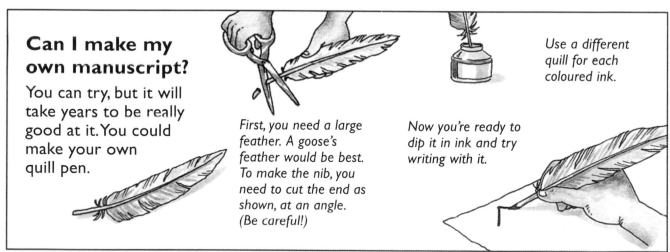

Can I make my own manuscript?

You can try, but it will
take years to be really
good at it. You could
make your own
quill pen.

First, you need a large
feather. A goose's
feather would be best.
To make the nib, you
need to cut the end as
shown, at an angle.
(Be careful!)

Now you're ready to
dip it in ink and try
writing with it.

Use a different
quill for each
coloured ink.

What was a joust?

A mixture between a mock battle and a fun day out. Knights would fight each other on horseback in front of cheering, and booing, crowds. The knights weren't supposed to kill each other, but sometimes they did by mistake.

What was "trial by combat"?

This was when two knights actually meant to kill each other, as an official way to settle an argument. This shouldn't be confused with a joust.

A pickpocket

A trumpeter

The lord of the castle

A crown of laurels for the winner

The herald. His job is to call out the names of the knights in each contest.

These seats have the best view of the action. The richest and most important people are in here.

A dancing bear

This guard is watching the joust when he should be keeping an eye out for trouble.

These entertainers are hoping people will throw them some coins.

Did they have prizes?

Yes, but they weren't usually valuable. However, the winner would be offered the loser's armour and horse, which could be very valuable. He could either keep them, or sell them back to the loser. Some knights made a living this way, going from joust to joust.

An archery contest

Ale tent

Wrestlers

This knight was hurt earlier on in the day. His injury isn't as bad as he thinks.

This priest is speaking out against the joust, because people might be hurt.

These dogs are having a fight of their own.

These peasants don't get seats to sit on or a canopy over them.

A short jousting lance. Some lances were much longer.

A charging knight

A marshal watching the contest

A poor beggar

The charging knight's charger

Did they have a referee?

Yes. He was called a marshal. It was his job to make sure that everyone played by the rules and didn't cheat.

25

How were castles defended?

Very well in most cases. Castles were built for defence and were hard to attack. They had high stone walls, small windows, and battlements for soldiers to hide behind.

Some even had deep moats full of water all the way around them, and a drawbridge that could be pulled up.

This scene shows the second day of the attack on this castle. The artist has cut away part of the tower so you can see inside.

Battlements

Machicolations. Rocks and rubble will be dropped down from here onto the enemy.

This iron gate is called a portcullis It can be raised or lowered.

Battering ram for knocking down the gate. If they can cross the moat, that is.

Catapult

The drawbridge is up to keep out unwanted visitors.

Sinking soldier.

These large wicker shields are to protect them from things thrown or fired from the castle.

Did they really pour boiling oil on the enemy below?

No, it was too valuable, although they may have used boiling water. They definitely threw rocks out of holes high up in the battlements, called machicolations.

What was a siege?

When an attacking army tried to stop anyone getting into or out of the castle. Once the food ran out, the people inside would either have to starve to death, or give up and surrender.

26

This leg has just kicked away the ladder.

The attackers at the top of the siege tower are running onto the battlements.

These extra defences were built weeks ago. The lord knew trouble was coming.

A dropped crossbow

Going down

Brave soldiers

Arrowslit windows. Just wide enough to fire out of. Very difficult for the enemy to fire into.

A siege tower, full of soldiers, has been wheeled up to the wall.

A tunnel, held up with wooden props, has been dug under the wall by the attackers. They are now burning the props. This should make the tunnel cave in and the wall fall down — they hope.

Rocks for firing

A larger slingshot catapult

What weapons did an attacking army use?

Plenty, and many of them are shown on this page. These include catapults, siege towers and also battering rams.

What was a battering ram for?

Ramming into doors and gates to smash holes for soldiers to get through. The very first battering rams were just logs.

Later, battering rams were put on wheels and covered over to protect the soldiers pushing them from being shot with arrows.

27

What were the crusades?

They were "holy wars", fought by Christians against the Muslim Turks, starting in the 11th century. They were called "holy" wars because the fight took place in the Holy Land, between people with different religious beliefs.

Why was there a war?

In the 11th century, the Arabs were conquered by a people called the Seljuk Turks. They made the visiting Christians unwelcome, and made them pay to visit Jerusalem. As a result, armies of Christian crusaders marched to Jerusalem to try to take it over.

Where is the Holy Land?

In what is now Israel, Jordan and Lebanon. Before the crusades, Christians went there to visit the holy city of Jerusalem, which was ruled by the Arabs.

This crusader was wounded in battle.

This scene shows a group of crusaders back in Europe. They've brought some wonderful things back with them from the Holy Land.

This beautiful carpet is a treasured possession.

This dog is pleased that his master is back home again.

Spices such as nutmeg and cloves came by sea and by land from the East Indies. They could cost as much as gold.

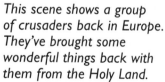

Kingdom of Jerusalem

HOLY LAND

Who won?

The crusades lasted over 200 years. The Christians won Jerusalem... then lost it again. In the end, all the lands around it were recaptured by the Turks.

The coloured areas on this map show Christian states set up in the Holy Land by the crusaders.

Did you know?

Crusaders brought back silks, perfumes, sugar and spices from the Holy Land. They also brought back new types of fruit, such as apricots, lemons, figs and dates.

There are many legends about the crusades,
and about one man who was said to be as
brave as a lion. He was the King of England.
His name was Richard the Lionheart.

The Minstrel and the Lionheart

Richard the Lionheart had fought for two long, hard years in the Holy Land. His knights had won many battles, thanks to his skill and bravery, but the city of Jerusalem was still in enemy hands. It was held by the Muslims, who were led by the mighty Saladin. Meanwhile, the French crusaders had gone home and King Richard had heard rumours that his brother was plotting with the French King to seize the throne of England

Richard agreed three years' peace with Saladin, and soon set off back to England to sort out his troubles. But the journey homeward across Europe was every bit as dangerous as the crusades... And he disappeared.

The English court realized that their king must have been taken prisoner in Austria or Germany. But nobody knew which castle was Richard's prison. A man called Blondel, an old friend of the king, travelled to Austria to try to track him down.

Blondel was a minstrel. His job was to sing songs and tell stories. Years before, he and King Richard had even written a song together. It was this song that Blondel now sang outside every castle wall. One day, Blondel heard a voice joining in the singing from a castle tower and he knew he had found the king!

Blondel hurried back to England, where enough money was raised to pay for King Richard's freedom. Or so the legend goes. It's certainly true that Richard enjoyed music. It's also true that he was taken prisoner in Austria in 1192 and a massive ransom was paid for his release. But what of Blondel? Who knows? It makes a good story.

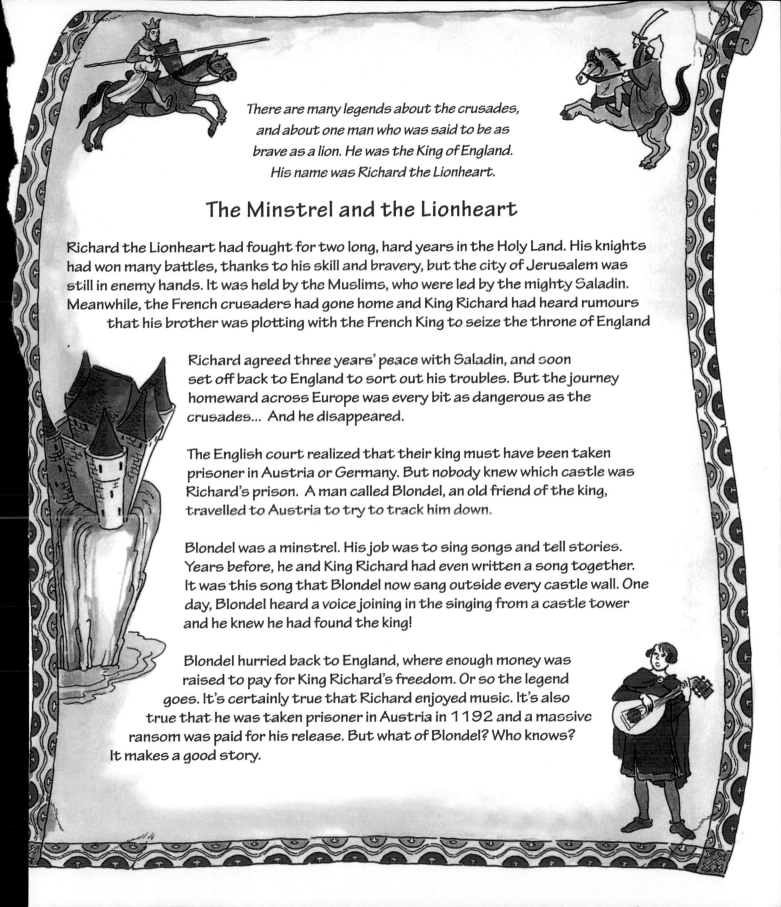

Where in the world are there castles today?

There are castles and fortresses all over the world. This map shows just a few of them. There are hundreds more.

Some castles are still lived in. Some are museums. Plenty of castles are open to the public, which means that you can go and look around them. Many castles are now in ruins.

In the Middle Ages, Germany was ruled by different warring princes. **Braubach** was one of many castles built in high, well-defended places all along the River Rhine.

ATLANTIC
OCEAN

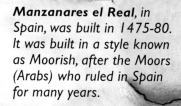

Manzanares el Real, in Spain, was built in 1475-80. It was built in a style known as Moorish, after the Moors (Arabs) who ruled in Spain for many years.

Krak des Chevaliers, in Syria, was rebuilt in the 12th century by warrior monks for the crusades.

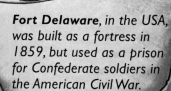

Fort Delaware, in the USA, was built as a fortress in 1859, but used as a prison for Confederate soldiers in the American Civil War.

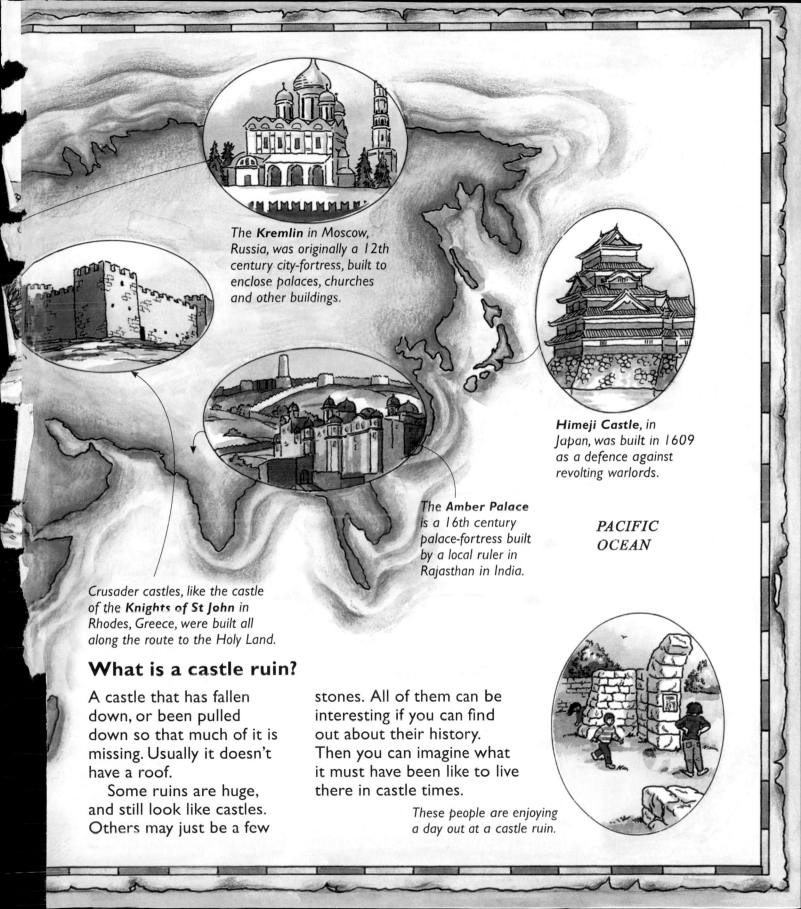

The **Kremlin** in Moscow, Russia, was originally a 12th century city-fortress, built to enclose palaces, churches and other buildings.

Himeji Castle, in Japan, was built in 1609 as a defence against revolting warlords.

The **Amber Palace** is a 16th century palace-fortress built by a local ruler in Rajasthan in India.

PACIFIC OCEAN

Crusader castles, like the castle of the **Knights of St John** in Rhodes, Greece, were built all along the route to the Holy Land.

What is a castle ruin?

A castle that has fallen down, or been pulled down so that much of it is missing. Usually it doesn't have a roof.

Some ruins are huge, and still look like castles. Others may just be a few stones. All of them can be interesting if you can find out about their history. Then you can imagine what it must have been like to live there in castle times.

These people are enjoying a day out at a castle ruin.

Index

Answers

Page 5.
*It collected at the bottom
of the chute. It smelled
terrible and could spread
disease.*

Page 15.
*An arrow fired from an
upright bow can travel
much further than one fired
from a crossbow. But an
arrow or bolt from a
crossbow is thicker and
strikes harder.*

This edition first published in 2015 by Usborne
Publishing Ltd, 83-35 Saffron Hill, London EC1N
8RT, England. www.usborne.com

Copyright © 2015, 1994 Usborne Publishing Ltd.
The name Usborne and the devices 🎈 are
Trade Marks of Usborne Publishing Ltd.